DR. KELLY
ARRINGTON-WILKINS

**HOW I
DISCOVERED MY**

**TRANSFORMED MY MIND
AND FOUND MY TRUE CALLING**

Cover & Design & Editing by Zelda Oliver-Miles

ISBN: 979-8-9905019-0-4 (paperback)
Printed in the United States

Published by Purpose4Living Consulting
Conyers, GA 3009
www.purpose4living.org

DEDICATION

Thank you, GOD, for the lessons, strength and your power within to break many generational circles of stances!

To my sister Valerie for beating the odds and maintaining sobriety for thirty-plus years. To my siblings, nieces, nephews and six generations to come, thank you for doing your best to beat the odds and change our history.

To my granddaughter Imani, you are my WHY that continues to lead me on this journey.

To my two King SUNs, Akeem and Thornton, it is because of you, I kept pushing past all the pain that catapult me into my Purpose, building a legacy for generations to come!

CONTENTS

ACKNOWLEDGEMENTS

To My Spiritual Mother/Leader, Apostle, Dr. Loretta V. Harris — thank you for seeing in me what I didn't see in myself. For being used by God to inform me that I was Chosen! Thank you for being obedient in October 2013 to speak in my life, 2015 using me to push me to step outside of my comfort zone to a level of Servant Leadership, Ordaining me as a Minister, and guiding me along the journey!

To the my Spiritual Daughters and Purpose for Living Partners, You know who you are. You have no idea how much Serving side-by-side with you and pouring into you truly helped build me up and strengthen me over the years! Thank you for believing, supporting, and serving with me.

A special, special thank you to my sister-friend, Prophetess Deborah (Vinise M. Capers), whom I danced with in the world and now dance for God together. I thank you for journeying with ME over the last 20 years and not judging my assignment because it looks different from yours.

Never forgetting where I come from:

My Plainfield NJ Village Sisters and Families- You know who you are!!!

The Late Reverend Kenneth Pittman and Family

Rosa & Walter Jones and my god-sisters, I learned so much of what to do and what not to do - independence, fun, family and forgiveness.

The Late Erma Morings (Jim)

Dawud & Shakurah Abdurrahman for being in the room when my son was born, walking me down the aisle on that first special day, being there when my first son was married, standing in so many gaps, and representing as my parents and children's grandparents always.

My Shero, Julia Porterfield, who planted those 1st seeds of entrepreneurship in me as a young girl.

My sister-friend, Pastor Tracy Shider (Husband Nate) of New Generation Worship Center in Plainfield, NJ, for showing me what true ministry, family, and marriage covenant looks like.

INTRODUCTION

Imagine dropping out of high school and then being in the boardrooms at big-shot Fortune 500 companies. Yep, that's been my journey. But I'm no superhero. I'm just a regular gal who decided to beat the odds by not letting my environment and circumstances dictate my life. I made the bold choice to chart my own course and embrace the power of faith and belief.

Through the pages of this book, you'll walk alongside me as I navigate the complexities of life, from growing up with drug addicts, being bullied, rejected, sexually exploited, abused, and falling dangerously in love. Not to mention dropping out of high school, becoming a single mom, and left to raise three younger siblings at nineteen when my mother died. Each chapter is a testament to the resilience of the human spirit and the unwavering belief that with faith, determination, and action, any obstacle can be overcome.

This book is more than just a recounting of my personal triumphs. It is a beacon of hope to inspire, motivate, and transition your thinking, especially if you find yourself in a stagnate place within your own personal wilderness. Within my story are insights and reflections of how I found my way through the wilderness and into the call on my life.

As early as thirteen, I developed strategic plans to move my life from a chaotic environment to one of calm, peace and tranquility even when life be lifing. I even had a plan for dropping out of high school. While I would not suggest doing it the way I did back in the 80s, I do encourage having a plan. Mine eventually led me to managing technical engineers, traveling to Japan, sitting in boardrooms, problem solving and transforming business operations for Fortune 500 companies. In addition, I became a serial entrepreneur owning several real estate properties, and businesses.

You will witness the transitions in my life that took me from seemingly looking like a person suffering to becoming a woman equipped with wisdom, common sense, and confidence. This book is formatted with chapters of real-life adverse situations that provides insight and pivotal points on the approach I took to overcome obstacle in addition, at the end of each chapter, you will find a reflective scripture and a questions intended to stimulate a deeper light to be shined within as you speak to your inner self transitioning your thinking to help get you closer to your Purpose4living.

So, brace yourself as you witness the determination, faith and works that built my muscle, and shaped me to be stronger in my faith, my mind, and purpose by recreating my narrative.

THE ROOT OF HER

HAVE YOU EVER RUMMAGED THROUGH THE REMNANTS of your childhood, seeking solace in the memories that emerge from the haze? My auntie and grandmother significantly influenced my few significant childhood memories. On weekends and breaks from school, they took me away from the chaotic lifestyle I was familiar with and introduced me to the essential aspects of a stable family environment. Because where and how I lived was a far from stable. The best part was that I got to be a kid.

The atmosphere at my aunt's place differed completely from that of my grandmother's. It was the early 70s and my aunt lived in the rough Prince Street projects in Newark, New Jersey. At auntie's place, I felt like a kid again because I could run to the candy truck on the corner and play with the other children in the building. Play often meant a game or two or three of spades in the stairwell. At five, I was one of the best players around. Any team I was on always won. It was here I developed critical thinking skills. Thinking about ways not to become a product of my environment.

When I wasn't playing with the neighborhood children, I hung out with my older cousins who showed me so much love, more than I received at home. Best of all, I never had to worry about dinner either. My auntie would make my favorite dishes, filling the house with the comforting aroma of macaroni and cheese or the savory scent of spaghetti with butter toasted bread.

My stays at my grandmother's house were very different. My grandparents lived on the east end of Plainfield, New Jersey, in a cozy two-story home that boasted a finished basement and a fenced backyard with lush green grass. They had a boat parked in the driveway next to an RV. They would take me camping in Cape May on the weekends in the RV with the boat in tow. To me, they seemed well off. Grandmother was a nurse; grandfather was a machinist at a local factory.

There were no children there for me to play with, so I spent a lot of time in the kitchen learning to cook; watching my grandmother take care of my grandfather. She would go to the back door and call him into dinner with such patience. She knew that he would be out there a little longer working on the boat or one of his "toys" before coming in to wash all the grease from his hands with his black soap that smelled like tar. It was like she timed it perfectly before placing our plates on the table. She enjoyed serving him.

They exposed me to the wonders of traveling and having a love for boats, opening my eyes to new experiences. They also instilled in me the value of a strong work ethic.

However, amidst the fond memories of my childhood visits to my aunt and grandmother's homes, there was a stark reality waiting for me at home where I went back to being the babysitter, housekeeper, cook, and even handling the food stamps to make sure there was food for me and my siblings before my mom spent it on drugs. There was always loud music, alcohol and drugs, verbal, and physical abuse in our apartment where I lived with my mother, four siblings and my mother's gay male best friend.

As a child, this was what fun, love, family, and community were all about. And the community loved my mother for her fun, laughter, wisdom to make money, and for always offering a couch to rest their heads on. I did not know how truly dysfunctional my life was.

Before I was twelve, I took care of my three younger siblings and myself, and I also handled the household budget. Our older sister disregarded us as she was dealing with pains that led her to get caught up in our environment. My mother didn't work, so we relied on the system and charity organizations to support us. I had to learn quickly to stretch a dollar and cook meals that would last us for two days. It was a real challenge with my mom's friends coming over every night and raiding the fridge.

With little help from any adult, I learned to survive with the basics. Not just for myself, but for my younger siblings, too. Back then, food stamps came in a booklet and looked like monopoly money. Each "food coupon" had a dollar value and was a certain color. For instance, a green coupon was $10 while a brown one was one dollar. I would hide an extra dollar or two in a shoe box or somewhere she would not look to ensure we could at least buy a loaf of bread in case fried bologna sandwiches were all we had for dinner. When we wanted something sweet to eat, I would make donut holes from leftover bread. We'd cut the ends off and roll the slices into balls, fry them, and roll them in sugar. We looked forward to those little treats.

I also looked forward to times I could go outside and play Double Dutch jump rope with the other girls. Sometimes I would walk over to the local-owned corner store where I'd buy candy with our food stamps. As embarrassing as that was, as a child, I found joy in it. Those trips were about the only time I enabled my mother's habits. I would buy 10 pieces of penny candy so I could get change. Food stamps couldn't be used to purchase alcohol or cigarettes. I'd take the 90 cents and buy my mother a 75-cent pack of Newport 100s.

Feeding us wasn't my only responsibility. I had to make sure me and my siblings got off to school every day and kept up with our schoolwork and grades. My grades were good even though I struggled with reading and word pronunciation. My penmanship was very poor, too. I couldn't grasp cursive writing; I didn't have much time to practice at home either. But, there were days I walked around wondering if people knew what was going on behind our closed doors. I mean, our apartment was "the hangout" spot.

Again, no one ever helped us, helped me. I made sure our clothes were clean to the best of my ability and that we didn't look unkempt. But I had feelings of shame and embarrassment.

Today, believe it or not, I am thankful for some of the unstable times because through all the grown folk mess I learned to dream in my immature, undeveloped mind. Dreaming kept me humble and grateful through those dark days, waiting with faith for moments of light, rescue, and refuge.

Use these takeaways and the questions that follow to embark on your own journey of self-discovery and resilience, drawing inspiration from my triumphs and lessons learned.

Pivotal Takeaways:

VALUE POSITIVE ROLE MODELS: Reflect on the positive influences in your life who provide stability and love amidst chaos. Seek out mentors or role models who embody the qualities you admire and then learn from their guidance and support.

RESILIENCE IN ADVERSITY: Recognize the strength within yourself to overcome challenging circumstances and find moments of joy. Practice resilience by focusing on solutions rather than dwelling on problems and seek support from trusted friends or community resources.

EMPOWERMENT THROUGH EDUCATION: Embrace the power of education as a tool for personal growth and transformation, despite financial hardship or a lack of parental guidance. Invest in your education and skill development and pave the way for a brighter future.

IMPORTANCE OF SELF-CARE: Prioritize self-care and emotional well-being, even amidst adversity, by finding moments of joy and refuge in simple pleasures and positive experiences. Practice self-compassion and seek out supportive relationships or activities that nurture your mental, emotional, and physical health, as the protagonist did through moments of play and connection with friends.

Thoughts of Purpose:
What is that one childhood moment that helped develop who you are today?

Can you identify how you turned a negative situation into a positive outcome?

What would you tell the younger version of you going through the same situation?

Scripture Reflection: Trust God from the bottom of your heart
"Trust in the Lord with all your heart and lean not on your own understanding; in all your ways submit to him, and he will make your paths straight."
(Proverbs 3:5-6, KJV)

TWO

LIVING IN LACK

As I grew into my pre-teen years, it was evident that my self-esteem was taking a hit. Not only did I feel embarrassed about our living situation and how we were barely getting by, but I also stood out physically from the other kids my age. My feet seemed to grow at an alarming rate, reaching an adult size 11 by the time I turned 11. My body was changing too — my backside spread wider, my skin turned darker, and my hair seemed to coil tighter because it was not appropriately managed. The teasing and bullying from the neighborhood children only made it worse.

I remember going home crying because of mean comments about my looks or getting hit for no reason. And then one day, my mom's friend, Sonny, did my hair in box braids and said I looked beautiful. He told me not to let anyone ruin my hair or come home crying. He told me something I'll never forget: if someone messes with me, I should stand up to them and not back down until they back off. And if they hit me, grab the one with the biggest mouth first.

The next day girls mocked me for finally getting my hair done, saying things like, "you think you cute cause you finally got your nappy head done." Sure enough, when I got off the bus that afternoon, a group of girls was waiting for me at the bus stop. Somehow, I found the courage to stand up for myself and follow Sonny's advice. I fought back with all the strength I had. And you know what? They never bothered me again after that.

That moment was a turning point for me. It showed me that I had the strength to stand up for myself and that I didn't have to tolerate bullying, verbal or physical abuse from anyone. Someone believed in me, and that belief ignited a newfound sense of self-esteem within me, empowering me to believe in my own strength and abilities.

In the neighborhood, I formed a few close friendships that have stood the test of time, and our connection continues to this day. These friendships were like a lifeline when my confidence was at its lowest. Their unwavering support provided me with a sense of comfort and reassurance, erasing the feeling of loneliness during my struggles. Their support not only boosted my confidence, but also filled my days with laughter, joy, and a comforting sense of safety.

During this period of self-doubt, I came to understand the importance of sisterhood. Having someone to confide in became crucial for me, and the friendships I formed provided solace during my darkest moments of need. Despite the hardships, the friendships I cultivated turned out to be a blessing in disguise. They taught me that true friends are the ones who stand by you, especially when times are tough.

Even when food was scarce and times were tough, I found moments of joy in the company of my newfound sister-friends. At the end of the month, when my mother was at home more often, I didn't have to shoulder as much responsibility, allowing me to spend quality time with my friends. While the last days of the month also brought financial strain and an empty fridge, having my sister-friends by my side made it feel like a gain rather than a loss.

The lack of proper parental guidance, love, and affection forced me into survival mode. It made me develop an inner fight for what I deemed important, yet it also made more vulnerable to faults. Despite the lack of guidance, I became responsible beyond my years, constantly planning and preparing for the uncertainties of tomorrow. The scarcity of resources, especially food, taught me to stash away a dollar or two today for bread tomorrow. This survival mentality shaped my thinking, making me perpetually cautious and risk adverse.

Little did I know then, this mindset would become a valuable skill in my adult life, a trait that others would go to school to learn. Every small victory, every meal on the table, was a cause for celebration during the chaos of drug addiction and instability. Every day I didn't have to see someone sitting at our kitchen table with a syringe in their arm shooting up heroin was a joyous day. Witnessing my sister come out of her room not looking depressed because she couldn't get high, was a good day. These moments fueled my determination to overcome obstacles and find joy amid adversity.

Use these takeaways and the questions that follow to embark on your own journey of self-discovery and resilience, drawing inspiration from my triumphs and lessons learned.

Pivotal Takeaways:
PRACTICE POSITIVE SELF-TALK: Replace negative self-talk with positive affirmations.

SET REALISTIC GOALS: Set achievable goals for yourself and celebrate your progress, no matter how small, along the way. This will build your confidence and reinforce your belief in your abilities.

SEEK SUPPORT: Reach out to supportive friends, family members, or mentors when you need encouragement or guidance. Surrounding yourself with positive influences can help bolster your self-belief and resilience.

SHOW GRATITUDE: Express gratitude for the supportive relationships in your life whether through words of appreciation or acts of kindness.

FIND JOY IN EVERYDAY MOMENTS: Find joy and gratitude in the small moments of life by focusing on the present moment, such as spending time in nature or enjoying a good meal.

KEEP A GRATITUDE JOURNAL: Write down three things you are grateful for each day. This will shift your focus from negativity to positivity and cultivate a mindset of gratitude.

LEARN FROM MISTAKES: Look at your mistakes as learning opportunities and opportunities for growth. Reflect on these experiences, identify the lessons learned, and use that knowledge to make future decisions and actions.

STAY POSITIVE: Try to maintain a positive outlook, even in the face of adversity. Focus only on the things you can control, practice self-care, and stay connected to supportive relationships to help them weather life's ups and downs.

Thoughts of Purpose:

When was the first time you can recall you felt a lack of confidence?

How did you overcome that feeling of lack or have you?

Did someone else contribute to that feeling of lack; if so, have you forgiving them?

Can you think of a time when you found joy during a time of lack?

Scripture Reflection: Help each other get stronger as believers.
"Wherefore comfort yourselves together, and edify one another, even as also ye do."
(1 Thessalonians 5:11, KJV)

THREE

IT TAKES A VILLAGE

As mentioned in the previous chapter, my family lived on the west end of town. The suburb neighborhood were mostly single-family homes and duplexes with apartments on top and bottom with a few side-by-side as well. We lived on the second floor of one of those duplexes; ours was a three-bedroom apartment with attic.

The families in my village were not like mine. There were probably more single moms raising their children alone in our village than there were two parent families. Even though there were some families with two parents at home, I didn't see the dad much. Some of those moms worked and used their skill sets while others relied on housing aid and welfare, and some even turned to sex, drugs, and alcohol like my mother. The moms that did work, worked hard every day to make sure their children had all the basics — a stark contrast from me having to take care of myself and my three younger siblings.

I, however, found solace and support in the families of my close friends; even the girls who once bullied me became my friends. These families introduced me to a new level of care, structure, and familial dynamics that contrasted sharply with the chaos of my own home life. I welcomed this additional layer of familial connection from the "village." They embraced me warmly, offering friendship, sanctuary, and a hot meal.

Our downstairs neighbor, whom I affectionately referred to as "auntie," was one of the kind-hearted, hardworking mothers who embraced me and whom

I learned from. She rarely came up, but she'd often call us down to see if we were hungry. Auntie was my shero. She was a single mother, who managed to balance work and raising a family unlike my mother. I'd watch her leave home, fashionably dressed, and head to work. After work she spent time planning and developing a transportation business. Her journey of starting and running her business, which is still going strong today, was like a light bulb turning on for me, fueling my curiosity and inspiring me to seek more knowledge, take more action, and strive for more.

Whenever she went on dates, she would often ask me to babysit her two daughters, despite all of us being roughly the same age. I guess that didn't matter because she knew that I was very responsible taking care of my younger sister and brothers, making sure they were fed and clothed. I was grateful for her. She didn't realize it, but she was planting seeds of professionalism and class in me. (Some years ago, on a return trip to the community, I had the opportunity to express my gratitude and thank her for the impact she had on my life.)

Auntie wasn't the only village mom that fed me or made an impact on my life. One of my friends lived at the end of the block; she was one seven children. There was always something good on the stove cooking, and I was always invited to dinner when I was on that end of the block. Another family, across the street, was where my bestie lived with her mom, grandfather and siblings. Her grandfather always offered us with treats and sent us to the corner store for him; he let us keep the change. These families gave me a glimpse of what a "normal" family looked like.

In one of the village homes lived a remarkable father who was raising two daughters. My younger sister often hung out with them, and I found great reassurance know she was under his watchful eye. This dad was kind, generous and firm. I felt at ease knowing that my sister would be under his watchful eye, as keeping her away from the chaos of our apartment as often as I could, was a priority for me. This father's discipline, structure and restrictions were welcomed by both of us because those were things we did not receive at home.

When I wasn't hanging out at my friends' houses, we'd meet up at the neighborhood community center to do homework, play games such as hopscotch and Double Dutch jump rope, and have fun on the playground. I even took boxing lessons there. We'd also get snacks after school.

THE PASTOR

At 13, a family within the village introduced me to a deeper connection with God. As a young girl, I always felt a strong sense of spirituality and relied on prayer for guidance. However, it was during this pivotal time in my life that I began to cultivate a stronger commitment and relationship with God. Despite the influence of my younger siblings' father, who practiced Islam, I remained steadfast in my devotion while navigating between the Mosque and the church with unwavering resolve. I knew I needed the faith instilled in me by my Baptist/Pentecostal family.

This village family had no idea what was happening behind the closed door of our apartment each time they picked me up or dropped me off. Each Sunday, they took me with them to a beautiful Sunday service in a small storefront church in Newark, New Jersey. This routine continued until the day the Pastor, who became a significant figure in my life and eventually my godfather, took a leap of faith and established his own storefront church in Plainfield. One Father's Day, however, I couldn't attend service, only to receive heartbreaking news after that my godfather died of a heart attack while delivering a sermon titled "Are you ready?"

In my grief, I found solace in knowing that he wouldn't have wanted to go any other way. I am forever grateful for my godfather, whose legacy impacted my life and the lives of many others he touched through his unwavering dedication to God's ministry.

Use these takeaways and the questions that follow to embark on your own journey of self-discovery and resilience, drawing inspiration from my triumphs and lessons learned.

Pivotal Takeaways:
COMMUNITY SUPPORT: The extended family that provides refuge and guidance when times get tough.

ROLE MODELS: Positive role models, such as "Auntie" and the village father, exemplified traits of resilience, professionalism, and discipline, inspiring personal growth and ambition.

SPIRITUAL GUIDANCE: Spiritual communities can provide a sense of belonging and guidance, shaping their moral compass and values.

RESILIENCE: When things get hard, finding comfort and inspiration in supportive communities helps you bounce back and overcome your challenges.

Thoughts of Purpose:

Where was your favorite go to place as a child?

What were the pivotal points in your life that led you to the path you are in right now?

Who are those people that molded your character and whose principles and behavior you have set yours from?

Scripture Reflection: Loving one another is obedience.
"Bear ye one another's burdens, and so fulfil the law of Christ."
(Galatians 6:2, KJV)

it takes a village

FOUR

LIVING IN THE WILDERNESS

HAVE YOU EVER FELT LIKE YOU WERE LIVING IN A WILDERNESS, surrounded by towering mountains and unseen threats? Feeling isolated and unable to trust anyone? Facing challenges as daunting as lions, tigers and bears? That's how I felt, but with unwavering faith and determination I pushed forward to overcome the generation curses that tried to hold me back.

I gained invaluable lessons in family dynamics, personal growth, and spirituality from my village. I discovered the importance of family structure, witnessed various familial dynamics, and nurtured a deeper relationship with God. Additionally, I embraced independence and unearthed my leadership capabilities, notably leading the youth choir—a role I didn't anticipate but cherished deeply.

Despite these enriching experiences, a sense of loneliness and distrust lingered, leading me to feel adrift in the wilderness, disconnected from the world around me. But I was determined to break free from the shackles of abandonment, low self-esteem, and a lack of familial love and structure. Confronting these challenges head-on, I battled against the grip of shame and rejection, determined to overcome the barriers that threatened to consume my spirit and lead to my spiritual demise.

The loneliness I experienced was, in part, a result of the chaotic environment at home. From as early as five, I witnessed my mother's friends doing drugs or succumbing to overdoses at our breakfast table. Then one day, walking inside from playing outside, I witnessed my mother's boyfriend sexually abusing a young girl in my mother's bed. I knew, in my seven-year-old mind that what I was seeing wasn't right, but somehow, I learned to block it out. By the time I was twelve, I'd learned to shoot heroin between my sister's toes because the veins in her arms and legs were blown out or collapsed. I'll never forget the time my sister was super sick, and I had to go to the corner drug dealer and ask for drugs on credit to keep her from dying. I had no fear because I had already been exposed to the conversations while being in the car, traveling out of town to pick up drugs, going up and down buildings of New York City where you could buy drugs cheaper and make three to four times profit.

I developed a strong sense of assertiveness and boldness at an early age to avoid what happened to my sister from happening to me. I was firm with my NO. I didn't know it then, but I believe my survival instincts activated within me, especially since my mother explicitly approved of the actions of certain men in the neighborhood, saying "it's okay to let (him) touch you" when she sent me to pick up her drugs or money for food. Her wanting to exploit me only fueled my determination to find a solution — a way out of my wilderness — to survive without bowing down to sex and drugs.

With each passing day, I planned and prayed even more. Then one night, as I prayed for a way out, I saw a commercial for Job Corps Center. The commercial said at Job Corps I could learn skills, a trade, earn a high school diploma and receive an allowance for free. The commercial spoke to me. I was only thirteen, but I started dreaming of ways I could go there; I couldn't enroll until I was sixteen. So, I planned.

Over the next three years, I focused on keeping my grades up. But I needed money to get to the Jobs Corps Center, so I had to find a job. A few of my neighborhood sister-friends, who were older, worked and I asked them to help me get a job where they worked. At first, they laughed at me because they knew

I was only thirteen, but they helped me anyway. I forced a birth certificate, lying about my age — it showed I was eighteen. I worked with them after school from four to midnight at a factory packaging candy and barrettes. Oftentimes, I didn't have a way home. I'll never forget taking a taxi home one night; we jumped out and ran down the street so the driver wouldn't know where we lived.

§ § §

While working was beneficial for me, it meant that my younger siblings, aged ten, seven, and four, were left alone with my mother and older sister, who was now twenty years old. Home was not a safe place for them. At fourteen-years-old, I had to think and act more maturely than the average teenager.

By now my mother's boyfriend/my younger siblings' dad had stopped coming around, which I was glad about. His presence often made me think about my father. Where was he and why he never came around? I remember asking my mom once and she said he lived in Newark New Jersey. It so happened that the church I attended was in Newark, New Jersey. I asked my godfather, who was also my pastor, if he would take me to the last address that my mother had.

I remember seeing his name on the mailbox and walking up the steps and knocking on the door. I knocked several times, but no one answered. When I got home, I told my mom that he didn't answer the door. Feelings of being unwanted began to creep in. I guess after thinking about it, my mother shared with me that my grandmother, my father's mother, lived in Jersey City and that the last address she remembered was on Communipaw Avenue. Jersey City is a bigger city than where we lived and an hour-long train ride, but I was up for the challenge.

This is the early 80s and when there were no cell phones, but at fourteen I am allowed to take a train to find my grandmother and my father. I make it to Jersey City safely and from there I took a taxi to the address my mother gave me. I ring the doorbell and a lady chewing snuff comes to the window. "Oh my God, are you, my granddaughter?" she asks. "I have not seen you since you were a baby." She never opens the door or invites me in. "Your daddy is probably up the street, two blocks up, at that bar," she said. Hopeful, I head toward said bar.

Because of my size, I looked older than my fourteen years, so I walked right into the bar, and nobody said a word to me. I spot the man that I was told was my birth father and walk over to him. "Look at my baby daughter," he said. He's drunk in the middle of the day. He stood and greeted me, introducing me to all his friends so proudly. He told me he loved me, but he didn't show it when it mattered most. At that moment, it was me getting back to the train to go home at night, alone. I so wanted him to take that long train ride back with me, keep me safe and make sure no one harmed me. This was my first brush with rejection and abandonment. How could he not make sure I got home safely? That's what I kept asking myself. Nevertheless, I got home safely and told my mother I had seen him. The visit didn't go as I hoped, but it taught me two things: shake off unmet expectations and pray and plan. I was going to beat the odds that were against me!

That long train ride gave me the courage and boldness to take another train to the Job Corps Center main office in Newark, New Jersey to find out all the steps I needed to ensure that I'd get into the program when I turned sixteen. Getting into Job Corps wasn't just about my survival. I was going to be able to come back and help my sisters and brothers. While the idea of leaving home excited me, I also found myself become more defensive, angry, and aggressive. Those emotions acted as a shield of protection because I stayed in fight or flight mode. Nothing was going to get in my way of going to Job Corps.

I never shared my plan with anyone — not my god-sisters, sister-friends, or my godfather. I just prayed about it. Fast forward to the day I went to get the paperwork and learn more about Job Corps. I'd saved money for my train ticket to Newark, New Jersey where their office was located. The recruiter gave me all the information I needed and told me that I'd need to get my mother's signature on the application. I returned home and went back to school the next day, to get forms I'd need to drop out of school. Desperate, I forged my mother's signature on the application and the forms for the school. (This is not a behavior I condone.) I went back to Job Corps to turn in my paperwork. They gave me my acceptance letter, but realized I was only fifteen. I had to wait four months before I could start the program. They did, however, let me select the location I wanted to attend. I picked the one furthest from home, and all the chaos, I could — Callicoon, New York.

My village gave me a going away party. It was hosted at my village auntie's home; she had a big house she purchased during a Dollar House program. She loved the neighborhood children and allowed us to hang out and she often let the neighborhood people that fell on hard time live there, too.

She was often upstairs and her kids smoked marijuana and drank there, so I knew the party would be wild but fun. One room of the house had people sitting in a circle smoking and one person dipped the marijuana in some type of fluid. Before I knew it my auntie was pouring milk down his throat to keep him alive.

So many friends were hurt by the drugs, alcohol and abuse. So many of them became stuck with lack of maturity in their minds, stuck in a mental prisons, drug dealers being put in prison with twenty and thirty years of life taken from them. So much trauma that I blocked out in order to push past the chaos and beat the odds that were stacked against me.

I finished the two-year program in eight months because I had already tapped into the leader in me and because I was used to doing things independently. Because I loved to sing in the church and stay the course with my faith, I became the leader of the Job Corps choir and we often presented plays and other activities for the attendees and community. During those eight months, I was truly in survival mode. The chaos at home taught me how to hustle and how to save. Our weekly allowance was $27.50, and it could be used for food or bus fare home. By the end of the week, I didn't have enough to leave campus, which was one of the things we had to do — leave on the weekends. I often went home with my roommate, who lived in Atlantic City. Her mother always gave her extra money for my bus ticket. As my way of repaying her, I cleaned and cooked when I got there. My roommate was a spoiled, only child, but I loved the relationship she and her mother had with each other.

I also did what I vowed I would never do and that is sell marijuana. I'm not proud to admit it now. But I did it for a few months to make extra money to survive campus life. It helped me keep my independence. With the money I made, I bought a hot plate and became the campus "happy hour cook." When everyone else was buying snacks, I went to the store and bought chicken, flour, and boxed macaroni and cheese. I sold hot, home-cooked dinner plates.

When I completed the program early, I moved to Atlantic City and lived with my roommate's mother while she still lived on campus. I was so grateful. At seventeen, I worked two jobs, helped my friend's mother and saved as much money as I could so that when I did return home, I could find a place of my own, but help my mother with bills and expenses.

After saving enough money, I moved back to my New Jersey hometown and got my own place and the unexpected happened. I met a guy, my first boyfriend; he helped me create a family structure for my younger siblings, who often spent time with me at my apartment. Even though my boyfriend was older, I helped him create multiple streams of income using his talents and skills. Together, we formalized and marketed two businesses – a construction company and DJ business we called "Small Touch." I made the very first set of business cards for both businesses.

I didn't shy away from the love and joy that came with family gatherings, music, cooking, and a little drinking of alcohol. Before I knew it, I found myself pregnant and the relationship turned abusive. I found myself staying with him hoping to show my younger siblings what stability in a relationship looked like. Deep down, I knew I didn't want to raise a child alone. So, I stayed. I realized that there is no stability in an abusive relationship. So, I began to pray and ask God for a plan of escape.

Sadly, my mother never held my son because I made up my mind that after my child was born, I would not take him inside that house. I drove by her house and asked her to come outside to see her grandchild, but she wouldn't. I gave birth to my son whom my mother never got to hold. I remember driving over to the house I grew up in and asking her to come outside but she wouldn't. So, like Mufasa did Simba, I held my son up toward the window and said, "meet your grandson."

Three months later, while on my way to church, our downstairs neighbor called me and said, "I think your mother is dead." My little brother, who was nine at the time, found her unresponsive when he went to ask her what was for breakfast.

I felt I didn't have a choice now but to put my escape plan into place. Nothing and no one were going to stop me from beating the odds of having a better life.

Use these takeaways and the questions that follow to embark on your own journey of self-discovery and resilience, drawing inspiration from my triumphs and lessons learned.

Pivotal Takeaways:

<u>FAITH AND DETERMINATION:</u> Unwavering faith and determination can provide the strength needed to overcome even the most daunting obstacles.

<u>RESILIENCE IN ADVERSITY:</u> Adversity can be a catalyst for growth and resilience. By confronting challenges head-on, one can emerge stronger and more resilient than ever before.

<u>STRATEGIC PLANNING AND SELF-RELIANCE:</u> Strategic planning and self-reliance are essential for navigating life's challenges and overcoming adversity. By setting goals and taking decisive action, individuals can chart their own course to success.

<u>SEEKING SUPPORT AND ESCAPE:</u> Seeking support and planning an escape route from abusive situations is crucial for breaking free from cycles of dysfunction and abuse. With determination and courage, one can overcome even the most challenging circumstances and build a brighter future.

Thoughts of Purpose:

Have you ever felt lost and lacked purpose?

How did you realize your purpose in life and how did you go about achieving it?

What were the eventual outcomes of your journey towards a purposeful life?

Scripture Reflection: God will provide whatever the need.
"Yea, they spake against God; they said, Can God furnish a table in the wilderness?"

(Psalms 78:19, KJV)

FIVE

LOSING TO WIN

LOSING A MOTHER AT NINETEEN left me grappling with an overwhelming sense of loss and responsibility. Yet, amid that loss, I embarked on a journey to transform my thinking and find a path to triumph.

I found myself taxed with the responsibility of caring for my brothers, aged fifteen and nine, while my sister was twelve. Additionally, I had a three-month-old child of my own. I didn't have much time to emotionally mourn because I had to quickly figure out a plan to keep them out of foster care. Luckily, I had a good job and some savings during this time of my life. But my sister and I still needed to scrape together money for our mother's funeral.

My mom tried to kick her drug habit. Back then they used to give addicts Methadone to reduce the cravings and withdrawals. Daily from a local clinic. I remember waiting in line with her at the clinic to get her dose only to spit half of it out into a small vial and sell it to a close friend. When my mom hit forty-eight, she developed asthma and had trouble sleeping at night.

One Saturday night, she called me, coughing bad. I asked if she wanted to go to the hospital, but she said no and just took her asthma medicine and went to sleep. Who would've guessed that would be the last time I heard her voice. She died in her sleep from walking pneumonia.

I remember the countless phone calls and endless visits to different organizations trying to scrape together enough money. My grandmother had already passed away, and my grandfather, Lewis gave what he could, but it still wasn't enough. My mother had three brothers, but unfortunately, two of them had been incarcerated for my entire life, and the other brother, who lived in New Orleans, wasn't close enough to provide us with any support.

We were really hoping my mom's sister, who helped raise me, would pitch in to help us, but she couldn't offer much help either. And unfortunately, my younger siblings' dad's side didn't step up either. We were really counting on our aunt and uncle to check in on us and lend a hand, but they hardly ever did.

Even though my older sister was very distant because of her addiction, I thank God for her as I watched her trying to turn her life around. She was holding down a job as a certified nursing assistant, and doing her best to raise her two children, aged five and two. My older sister and I became stronger than ever and a year after our mom passed away, I convinced her to go to rehab to turn her life around and help me. During what felt like forever, I looked after my niece and nephew, paid the bills to keep the lights on while she was gone, and went to work every day all while dealing with cheating, abusive boyfriend until I had him escorted out of my apartment.

After the loss of my mother, I had to quickly transition my thinking. No time for sorrow or grief. I had to hustle to secure housing and keep my siblings together and out of foster care. I had no idea that getting Section 8 housing would benefit me, my siblings, and future generations. So, without welfare or food stamps, I made enough to keep a roof over our heads thanks to housing assistance and $68 per child from social security, totaling $204 each month. It wasn't enough, but my sister and I did the best we could to keep the children fed and clothed.

Having already been working for a few years, I had purchased a new car, some stylish clothes, and a stable job, so they assumed I had it all. The idea of having more and living better was quickly diminishing because of the new additions. We were barely getting by as a family of six. My siblings felt that

I could do more to financially support them. Dealing with peer pressure was tough, but what made it even harder was the absence of a mother-figure in their life; even though they lived in chaos, they still had mom.

The toll of losing mom was different for each of my siblings. My oldest sister's life was saved, and a year later, she was able to overcome her addiction and support and care of our other siblings. My two brothers dealt with the loss in similar ways, letting their anger take over and land them in and out of prison. They didn't really know how to escape their own mental prisons. My older sister and I managed to protect and keep our younger sister away from the streets and drugs, but she never fully recovered from the pain and sense of being abandoned by both her parents.

Even with all the family drama, I managed to keep it together and help everyone succeed, hoping they'll overcome and win someday. I knew I had this one thing I had to conquer — getting out of that abusive relationship. I prayed and pleaded with God to break this cycle for my son. I didn't want him to think this behavior was normal, like I did when I saw my mom being abused. So, no drugs and no abuse in our house. I kept praying, and one day I came up with a plan to leave while going with my sister to get a Christmas tree. I already packed a small bag for my son and me and gave it to her ahead of time. On that day, I gave my landlord my thirty-day notice. I called Section 8 to transfer my voucher and sent my siblings to stay at my older sister's. I hid my son in Jersey City with my father and started searching for a new place to live.

Every day, he'd track me down, showing up at my friends' houses and even chasing my car, breaking the windows, yelling at me to come back home. I remember one time when I was trying to get away from him, I tried to jump in the car and pull off but he had my head out the window, bloody nose and begging him to let go of my hair. Later, after being harassed, stalked, and abused several times I called the police and they helped me move my furniture and clothes out. I knew I had to not allow this behavior to rub off on my son so when he got out of jail my aunt allowed him to live with her in New Orleans for awhile.

Finally, after four months, I found a new place for all of us to live together again. My younger sister was all over the place about moving, but in the end, she decided to stay with older sister. My older brother, who was eighteen, got caught up in the streets, selling drugs and robbing. He ended up with a sixty-six-year prison sentence. Going to prison saved his life (losing to win again), I think.

Despite having me as his guardian and my son as his nephew, my younger brother started feeling more abandoned. He started acting out and being defiant in school. I tried to leverage the local community centers and other youth programs, but nothing worked. One day, he was in school and somehow there was a child's toy bat in the classroom. The teacher asked him to put it away, but when she tries to take it from him, he accidentally let go and it hit her in the head. They took him to juvenile and the prison cycle continued. I knew I had to stop it with my son!

After a few years of working and being a single mom, I fell in love and had my second son's father at twenty-five. Having two children and helping raise my siblings, I knew I needed to make more money and wanted to do more in life. So, I came up with a plan to go to college and study business. The company I worked for gave tuition assistance, so I wanted to make the most of every opportunity.

It was rough, but I was determined to beat the odds of the generational cycles I once knew. I busted my butt every day, went to school three nights a week, supported my sister at her NA meetings twice a week, all while keeping a clean house, cooking meals, and trying to be good mom, sister, girlfriend, coworker, and friend.

I was always the voice telling people to think differently, chase their dreams, and prove everyone wrong. It was time to show others how they too could transition their thinking and beat the odds.

Use these takeaways and the questions that follow to embark on your own journey of self-discovery and resilience, drawing inspiration from my triumphs and lessons learned.

Pivotal Takeaways:

RESILIENCE IN ADVERSITY: In the face of loss and hardship, resilience is key. By embracing challenges head-on and refusing to succumb to despair, individuals can emerge stronger and more determined than ever.

STRATEGIC PLANNING AND RESOURCEFULNESS: Strategic planning and resourcefulness are vital for navigating crises. From securing housing to managing finances, proactive measures can mitigate the impact of adversity and pave the way for a brighter future.

BREAKING GENERATIONAL CYCLES: Breaking free from generational cycles requires courage and determination. By challenging ingrained patterns and fostering a mindset of growth and possibility, individuals can pave the way to their own path to success, despite the odds stacked against them.

SEEKING SUPPORT AND COMMUNITY: Seeking support from loved ones and community resources is essential during times of hardship. By leaning on others for guidance and assistance, individuals can find strength in unity and overcome even the most daunting obstacles.

Thoughts of Purpose:

Is there an ideal way to dealing with the loss of a loved one?

What individual options are you prompted to exploit whenever hard times strike?

Does challenges often drive you to a purposeful end?

Scripture Reflection: The Lord hears those who are discouraged, crushed, and in our darkest moments.

"The righteous cry, and the LORD heareth, and delivereth them out of all their troubles. The Lord is nigh unto them that are of a broken heart; and saveth such as be of a contrite spirit." (Psalm 34:17-18, KJV)

SIX

PAIN TO PURPOSE

IMAGINE STANDING AT A PIVOTAL MOMENT IN YOUR LIFE, torn between familiarity and the unknown. At this time, I realized that I never really knew what love looked like.

Then, I met mister handsome and charismatic, my second son's father. We were quite the couple in our little town. Once again, being the helpmate, what I now call the "purpose partner" that I am, the entrepreneur mindset I have rose up and we began to talk about our goals of owning unisex barber and beauty salons, hosting events and upscale hair shows. During this time, I had already given him his first set of clippers so that he could become one of the best master barbers in town. We'd started gathering the community and hosting upscale events, hair competitions and fashion shows to give the community something positive to look forward to. We did well financially until one night at the end of a show things turned bad; an altercation broke out and it left a few people injured, leading to a lawsuit against me and my company. The incident was all over the news. It could have changed the trajectory of my life BUT GOD. After taking the $6,000 we made that night to retain a lawyer, I ended up defending myself with God on my side. Not one person showed up for court to support me.

In addition to all of that the cheating, lying and deceit began. But being the determined person that I was, I wasn't about to settle for that kind of abuse again, so I decided to choose me and not expose my sons to this behavior, I left. Now I'm a single mom with two children, ages six and one.

I kept pushing through and refused to let my circumstances control my future. I worked hard and got promoted at work, while also keeping my grades up and staying in school. I'm so thankful for the babysitters who supported me. One day, as I was praying and thinking about how to make more money, I realized that I could invest in real estate someday. I thought it would be a good idea to take a real estate course while in college because I saw how important it is when looking for my own place. I remember saying one day I am going to be a landlord who gives housing to anyone, even if they don't have Section 8. I took the course just to learn about buying and investing, not because I wanted to sell houses. The goal was to become a landlord before I turned thirty.

So, while on Section 8, I saved and saved and saved. A few years later, at twenty-seven, I met a man that truly saw the deeper side of me as a gift and we fell in love. He was twenty-four and professional with a two-year-old daughter. My sons were eight and two and I was helping raise my siblings. He was good to me and I to him. We began to build a strong foundational relationship. We both loved God and often discussed our dreams, goals, and desires. When I told him about my dream of investing in real estate and he shared his dreams, too. Before we knew it, our dreams aligned. After three years, he asked me to be his wife and I said yes. We saved and saved as we planned. I'll never forget when I wrote the letter to Section 8 after we closed on the house. I thanked them for their program assistance and told them I was getting ready to buy a house and get married. Their help kept my family together and helped us beat the odds.

Two weeks after buying the first house, I already had tenants with signed leases. We leveraged the rent and security deposits and used them as down payment for another three-apartment house. We never moved into either of those houses. The plan was to save, and after a year, we'd buy our dream home in Poconos, Pennsylvania. Even though we both worked sixty miles away in New Jersey. We agreed to make the sacrifice to ensure we beat the odds.

The Poconos was a beautiful resort area with great schools and after school activities, including snowboarding. There weren't many people of color living there at that time. I always knew my boys would be safe, get a great education, and have a better life than me. So, this was the plan, and I just had this feeling that God was telling me I could totally do it. I was confident and wise enough to make it happen.

I had to see the dream with my eyes wide open. But before I could head to Pennsylvania, I had to check in on my sisters, niece, and nephew. I told my sister about my plan to move and asked her what she wanted in life. She said she didn't want to stay in New Jersey anymore. We chatted about her living in Tampa, Florida. I prayed and started figuring out how to help her with this transition. I was super excited to look for an affordable home for my sisters, planning my destination wedding and looking for a home in Pennsylvania for my family.

But not long after our conversation about her moving to Tampa, tragedy unexpectedly struck our family. My younger sister and cousins were involved in a devastating car accident that resulted in their hospitalization. My youngest sister lay motionless in a coma for a grueling two weeks before ultimately passing away. Even though my wedding was just weeks away, I had to pause and plan a home-going service for my little sister. I didn't cancel my wedding or postpone our move. I don't know how I got through all of that. Until the writing of this book, I realized I had blocked out these six weeks of my life.

A month later, in fight or flight mode, I initiated the purchase of my older sister's home in Tampa and set up five job interviews for her at area nursing homes. I even wrote her resignation letter for her current job. She totally trusted my transition planning, so as soon as she got off the plane, she became a homeowner. She couldn't even believe it when I handed her the keys to her dream house. It felt amazing to help my sister move out of New Jersey and start a new chapter of her life as I started a new chapter of my own.

After a few years, we upgraded and purchased a dream home in the Poconos. Our marital home was starter home with four bedrooms, three full bathrooms, a pool and a Florida-screen patio that we added a six-person hot tub to. We rented out our first home to a sister-friend and her family before later selling it.

Life was good. My oldest son was in college and both my youngest son and bonus daughter were headed to high school. We met most of our goals and heart's desires. We were sharing with our families, loved ones, and the community, until one day, my husband comes home with exciting news of getting the promotion that he worked hard for. As we celebrated, he told me the bad news of his shift change, which would mean a shift in our home routine. We talked about it and agreed not to let the commute or shift affect our relationship as we witnessed happening to other families. Being the forward thinker that I am, I start to imagine how his new hours and days off would impact us. This lasted for about a year until one day the communication shifted and I started feeling like a single mom running the property management business New Jersey and Pennsylvania alone with no support. It was a lot to handle. I had to take on more responsibility at home, with my oldest son in college, the youngest in middle school, and I'm juggling college part-time and a daily commute to work in New Jersey. Besides keeping the house clean, and paying the bills, I also had to make sure my sister got the support she needed to stay clean.

My husband was there financially, but not present mentally or physically. He stopped coming to school football and basketball games and began to spend more time in New Jersey after work than he did at home. After eight years of marriage, we divorced. After my marriage ended, I had to make some tough decisions to figure out what was best for my son, who was about to start high school. My eldest son was already in Raleigh, North Carolina on a football scholarship, so I thought it would be a great time to leave the cold Pocono Mountains for a warmer state like North Carolina.

Not making this transition would have meant enduring treacherous winter storms on my daily commute to work, all while trying to navigate the challenges of being a single parent. I made the bold decision to leave my high-paying job and take a leap of faith. I paid all the bills by myself, after my husband moved out, and after all the deposits for a new place, hiring a moving company, and everything else, I had no savings left. I moved with the rolls of quarters that I had carefully stashed away in a shoe box. This happened after the real estate market crashed, and we had to sell our last property for way less than what we paid. I had to deal with the IRS because we ended up owing them money. Meanwhile, I accepted a six-month contract. Every two weeks, like clockwork, I would request one or two rolls of quarters from the bank teller. This was my sustenance until I finally received my first paycheck and began my fresh start in Raleigh/Durham. That contract turned into a ten-year career and I completed my bachelor's degree.

Moving to Raleigh on a Thursday and making sure I was in a church on that Sunday is something I'll never forget. The pastor was preaching about our gifts and talents. He told us to dig deep and figure out what our gifts and talents are. "If you see yourself doing something that you enjoy for free, then that's most likely your purpose," he said. It dawned on me that all the transitions I've gone through and the help I've provided to others are a real gift. And if I had to give it away, I'd do it for free. That's when I realized transition planning was my calling.

I remember searching for steps to become a coach and all the schools I found were geared toward "for profit" companies. I took that additional training to become a certified professional coach. While continuing to work as an IT Project manager, I followed my personal dream of starting a nonprofit company, called Purpose4Living Inc I'd use my years of project management skills to help others transform their lives and beat the odds.

The instructor gave me a crazy look when I said I wanted to do coaching as a nonprofit. She reminded me that all the training materials we would be using were for profit companies. I told her I understood, but I would take everything she was offering and pivot it into nonprofit.

With my experience as a project manager in corporate America and going through different transformations myself, I became skilled at improving processes to turn dreams into reality. I did this by tapping in, brainstorming to figure out what needed to be done, making action plans, creating road maps, setting schedules, and getting rid of obstacles. These were skills I used in my own transformations and had already helped so many through theirs. These skills have been helpful in assisting others with their transformations from going back to school to life after divorce. But I specialized in transformations and building confidence, teaching others how to beat the odds, overcome challenges and avoid a stagnant life.

The pain I experienced pushed me to reflect and seek guidance from God, praying He reveal my purpose to me. As I started exploring my gifts and talents, I realized that my natural ability to motivate and help those in transition was a skill highly sought after by many. As my gift quickly made room for me, the doors of financial restoration swung open. A real estate opportunity that would allow me to offer much needed transitional housing was presented to me.

Time flew by, and before I knew it, my youngest son was entering his senior year of high school. My eldest son had already graduated college and was thriving as a police officer. I made the decision to shift my focus on myself. I began to envision my transition, which involved downsizing from a house to a smaller apartment. This would not only lighten my load but also cut down on expenses. I also perceived that this would guide and motivate me to make further sacrifices in my pursuit or resuming purchasing and investing in real estate again. God quickly reminded me of the way I entered the real estate business — purchasing an investment home first. I listened and followed instructions. I went looking for a multi-family residence that could be used as low-income housing to assist people in transition. I saved every dime from rent like I did before, and in a year, I could buy my own house.

With perseverance and strategic planning, I pursued education and career advancement, laying the groundwork for a brighter tomorrow. Recognizing the potential of real estate investment, I embarked on a journey to financial independence, leveraging opportunities and aligning with my aspirations.

Use these takeaways and the questions that follow to embark on your own journey of self-discovery and resilience, drawing inspiration from my triumphs and lessons learned.

Pivotal Takeaways:

VISION AND PLANNING: Having a clear vision for the future and crafting a strategic plan are essential for overcoming obstacles and achieving goals. By setting objectives and taking deliberate steps toward them, individuals can turn dreams into reality.

ADAPTABILITY AND RESILIENCE: Life is unpredictable, and resilience is crucial for navigating unexpected challenges. By remaining adaptable and resilient in the face of adversity, individuals can overcome setbacks and emerge stronger than before.

SEEKING OPPORTUNITIES AND LEVERAGING RESOURCES: Opportunities are often disguised as challenges. By actively seeking opportunities and leveraging available resources, individuals can unlock new possibilities and achieve success against all odds.

EMPOWERING OTHERS AND GIVING BACK: Success is not only measured by personal achievements but also by the impact on others. By empowering and supporting those in need, individuals can create a ripple effect of positive change, enriching lives, and communities.

Thoughts of Purpose:

Have you ever met situations that forces you to decide to lose to pave way for some other uncertain breakthrough?

What were the available options to be weighed?

Is it obvious that every failure amount to success in the end?

Scripture reflection: No matter how hard the situation, God has your back.
"Is there not an appointed time to man upon earth? are not his days also like the days of an hireling? As a servant earnestly desireth the shadow, and as an hireling looketh for the reward of his work: So am I made to possess months of vanity, and wearisome nights are appointed to me. When I lie down, I say, When shall I arise, and the night be gone? and I am full of tossings to and fro unto the dawning of the day." (Job 7:1-4, KJV)

SEVEN

OPENED DOORS

IMAGINE STANDING AT A CROSSROAD where resentment and forgiveness collide. That's where I found myself, standing at the crossroads of forgiveness and healing, as I made the difficult choice to forgive my youngest son's father for more than $100,000 in back child support. This pivotal moment paved the way for a new chapter of hope and reconciliation, not just for me but for my son as well.

Over the years, I've come to realize that forgiveness is the key that unlocks doors, allowing me to conquer my challenges and propel me toward my purpose. I learned that instead of fixating on the issues in front of me, it is more effective to turn to prayer and seek God for solutions and strategies. It wasn't easy, but I forgave those who hurt me, including my mom, and accepted that she was sick and did the best she could.

I had to forgive myself for the poor choices I'd made over the years. I had to pray and ask God for forgiveness for hurting those my decisions may have negatively impacted like my sons. Once I forgave myself, I had the courage to ask my sons for forgiveness. This was the key that unlocked the right door and gave me the strength, confidence, and straggles to better serve others.

When reflecting on the profound effects of forgiveness, one example stands out in my mind. It involves my decision to forgive my eldest son's father, despite the physical abuse I experienced when we were together. This act of forgiveness not only helped me heal, but it also led me to take our granddaughter to meet him for very first time when she was four. I will always remember that day. I'd heard he was going through a rough time after his marriage ended, so when I was in New Jersey, I went by to visit him with his granddaughter hoping to cheer him up and pray for and with him. Months later, he called and thanked me for praying for him. He said the prayer gave him strength and opens a new door of opportunity for him. When I forgave him, it was for me because I know God's word says unless I forgive, I can't be forgiven. But forgiving him, set him free, too.

To the matter of my youngest son's father. When I forgave my youngest son's father, it set me free. My son was seventeen, going off to college, and even though the law said he should get financial support, I decided to close that door to try and build a better relationship between father and son. My hope was that closing that door would take off the financial pressure, so he could offer support voluntarily. I sent his father a copy of the dismissal request that was sent to Family Court, saying I forgive him and relieve him from any future financial obligation and back pay.

I said that from now on, just like it says on our bills, 'in God we trust.' Although his father expressed gratitude and thanked me, I still forgive him and still pray for the healing of that relationship. Days after the dismissal, new doors began to open for me as I walked into who God called me to be in ministry: a vessel to "help restore families back to great abundance" (Isaiah 40:31, KJV). It had to start at home. If I had forgiven my son's father and apologized to my sons, what a difference it could have made if I had done it sooner.

With the decision to purchase a new investment property in the works, I believed the sacrifice would pay off, because I already had a blueprint and proof that it worked back in 1999; I saved every dime and buy a home for myself after a year. I was blessed to find a real estate opportunity in Raleigh to purchase a triplex and provide housing for those who were often denied. My first tenant was a young lady who had been sleeping in her car. Her daughter was living with one of her teachers; the teacher went above and beyond, jeopardizing her career for the little girl. Despite her less than stellar credit, previous eviction, and inability to pay a security deposit or utilities, I accepted her application. This young lady underwent what I considered my beta test for my nonprofit company. I let her pay partially to move in with a payment plan, and I kept the utilities in my name until she could transfer them into her own and stand on her own two feet. This young lady diligently returned to college, completing her degree while sticking to her budget, enabling her to save a significant amount of money to fulfill her dream of becoming a homeowner. When she left the "Raleigh North Carolina House of Purpose," she left behind her washer, dryer, and microwave, with the intention that they would bring blessings to the next tenant.

After making the difficult decision, I closed the door to my beautiful penthouse apartment and actually moved into one of the units within the triplex on the Southside of Raleigh-Durham. Many of those that knew me looked at me as if I was losing her mind, but I stepped out on faith and believed what I felt in my spirit which was to move into one of the units. Again, the goal was to sacrifice and save to buy myself a home within a year.

But four months later, I found myself transitioning through another not-so-great situation. I lost my six-figure job. With only a $350 weekly unemployment check, I had to carefully budget every expense. Looking back on it all, I realized that God had been preparing me for this moment, and I felt a deep sense of gratitude. I was a homeowner and didn't have to pay rent. It was in that moment I realized that obedience was greater than sacrifice. My thinking shifted to gratitude when it looked like the door had been shut. Thanking God for his guidance and giving me an ear to hear and faith to believe that moving in was the right thing to do despite what everyone else was saying.

After a five-month job search and experiencing humbling moments that reminded me of how far God had brought me, I continued to pour my efforts into the investment property, making sure it was comfortable for the new tenants in transition. Then God moved. A job offer came through offering a higher salary and a promotion in title.

But it didn't stop there. Another door opened and I was asked to speak at an event in Georgia. The topic I chose was "Birthing Purpose: Using what You Got." The memory of being on the plane, heading back, contemplating how God stretched me out of my comfort zone is forever ingrained in my mind. As I thought on those things, I heard a soft voice speak to me, telling me to start looking for my single-family home in Georgia. That evening, when I went to bed, I obeyed the voice and started looking for home in Georgia. I called about this one house and got a call back from the Realtor almost immediately. We ended up talking on the phone for two hours. God allowed me to minister to her. The next day, the Realtor called and said I was officially approved for a mortgage in Georgia. A year and six months later, God's manifestation revealed itself and my primary home in Georgia was beyond my prayers. God made it happen and I got the keys to my home now called the "House of Purpose - GA." I did not realize what God was up to, but He strategically separated me from everyone to draw me closer to Him.

For the first two years, my home served as a retreat for women in transition. They could come here to relax, recharge, heal, and plan for their future. These offering were all about expanding to serve my nonprofit organization, Purpose4Living Inc., and its mission.

Purpose4Living Inc.'s mission is to help women and particularly men through their transitions and empower them back up to be the Kings, Fathers and providers they were meant to be. This approach would let them regain their confidence and allow women to shed the personas they've had to adopt for so many years. This allows women to regain their positions and let go of all the testosterone-fueled mentalities we had to develop to survive. Ultimately, restoring and strengthening men, women and families back to great abundance.

As I continue to walk this path of purpose and healing, I am reminded of the importance of forgiveness in unlocking doors and ushering in new beginnings. In embracing forgiveness, forgiving myself and others, and asking for forgiveness even if it's not accepted, I found me and why I am the way I am designed; I found liberation and new opportunities. Despite facing setbacks, including the loss of my job, husband or friends, I persisted in my journey, guided by faith and gratitude knowing that God is a strategic God and He truly has the plan. Through obedience and sacrifice, I navigated through turbulent waters, eventually finding myself blessed with uncommon favor, unexpected blessings, and divine interventions.

Use these takeaways and the questions that follow to embark on your own journey of self-discovery and resilience, drawing inspiration from my triumphs and lessons learned.

Pivotal Takeaways:

EMBRACE FORGIVENESS: Recognize the transformative power of forgiveness in overcoming past hurts and fostering reconciliation. Practice forgiveness towards others and yourself, freeing yourself from resentment and bitterness.

SEEK DIVINE GUIDANCE: Turn to prayer and seek divine guidance when facing challenges and making difficult decisions. Trust in a higher power to provide clarity and direction in your journey towards healing and purpose.

PERSIST WITH FAITH: Despite setbacks and obstacles, persist in your journey with faith and gratitude. Maintain resilience and obedience, knowing that every challenge is an opportunity for growth and unexpected blessings.

EMPOWER OTHERS: Extend a helping hand to others in their transitions, empowering them to reclaim their confidence and embrace their true purpose. Through acts of service and support, foster healing, and transformation in the lives of those around you.

Thoughts of Purpose:

Do you believe that forgiving someone is for you?

Do you take moments to be still to hear from God?

Do you feel that Obedience better than a Sacrifice? Why or Why Not?

What have you done that pushed you beyond your comfort-zone and it turn out to be a victory?

Scripture reflection: Just believe
"Therefore I say unto you, What things soever ye desire, when ye pray, believe that ye receive them, and ye shall have them. And when ye stand praying, forgive, if ye have ought against any: that your Father also which is in heaven may forgive you your trespasses." (Mark 11:24-25, KJV)

EIGHT

STEPPING OUT

PICTURE THIS: YOU'VE RECEIVED THE GREEN LIGHT for a life-changing decision, but instead of shouting it from the rooftop, you keep it to yourself. Why? Because sometimes, the most profound transformations happen in silence. Being silent and obedient to whatever God says takes silence, so you can hear only His voice. Navigating the gray areas of life by faith takes faith, focus, works and action. Believing for the favorable outcome is NOT easy. It doesn't always feel good, but we must just TRUST!

After receiving the financial approval for the house in Georgia, I decided not to tell anyone — not my sons, my sister, or friends. I'd received some negative feedback about buying the triplex and moving in to one of the apartments because they couldn't see the vision. I decided to let God and let Him navigate me through this process. I was stepping out on faith and trusting Him. I coach people through this process daily and my blueprint says to seek employment in the new location before you move. I perceived God telling me to step completely out on faith and do the opposite — I purchased the house without knowing if I would be able to secure work or work remotely. This was in 2016 when working remotely was not that popular.

I went to my manager and HR and requested to work remotely. Whether they said yes or no didn't matter. I was being obedient and trusting God while preparing to start a new chapter in Georgia. The Realtor I was working with understood what I wanted in a home and sent lots of videos and pictures of different properties. Meanwhile, I submitted my letter to Human Resources outlining my request to become a home-based remote employee. This would mean I could work from my Atlanta home. This was approved by HR, as it was a condition from the mortgage company to secure the mortgage.

My search for a home finally ended, and I was amazed by the spacious layout — it was more than I imagined. As if things weren't challenging enough, a new obstacle emerged. The listing Realtor attempted to hinder the sale. Despite my offer being received before anyone else's, the listing Realtor got the homeowner to accept a different contract. I earnestly prayed about it believing and trusting God to work things out. Two weeks later, my Realtor called to say that "other offer" fell through and if I was still interested the house was mine. The paperwork was started immediately. It was uncommon favor.

But that wasn't the end of the obstacles; they seemed to multiply with each step I took. The week after I get the okay on the house, my supervisor calls me into the office and informs me that my approval to work remote was rescinded. The company made it clear that to remain a full-time employee, I would need to maintain a primary residence in North Carolina unless I chose to transition to a consultant role.

I made the decision to move forward with my plans to buy the house in Georgia, ensuring that it would serve as a secondary vacation home while I maintained my primary residence in North Carolina. I continued to believe God for the ability to work remotely from Georgia as I made some big sacrifices. Closing on the house in Georgia, I flew back and forth weekly, sometimes bi-weekly. I kept a second car and a suitcase of clothes in the trunk. For two years, I sacrificed and believed God for a full-time, work-from-home remote position. Exhausting more than my planned budget, flying back and forth, I made the most of my house in Georgia by renting it out for women's retreats and organizing scholarship events for those who've overcome adversity.

Once again God manifested His promise to me.

This entire transition and stepping out on faith felt like a harmonious alignment with my purpose. It enabled me to serve others and support them in navigating their own transitions to transform their lives. My own testimonies resonated with the path I was walking towards fulfilling my purpose. I was determined to continue walking in my purpose, regardless of the financial constraints or any other obstacles I may have faced.

God answered my prayers — I got a promotion in a new company, which not only increased my finances but also improved my work/life balance by giving me the option to work remotely. The interesting thing about this story is that here we are in 2024, and working remotely has proven to be beneficial and now is a norm. It's what I've been doing since 2016. Faith and perseverance helped me navigate the transitions in life and not only find but walk in my purpose.

Reflecting on why I wanted to explore the idea of "birthing purpose," I uncovered a deeper truth. Every twist and turn, every closed door or opportunity, every act of forgiveness has pushed me to move forward, encouraging me to step out of my comfort zone and go beyond to reposition posture and to never stop sowing into others and birthing purpose.

As I share the message within these pages, I am keenly aware of the profound impact it can hold for those that receive it. Doing the work to tap deep within and connect with my own life story inspired me to fully face any fears and embrace my purpose. By doing the work to heal, forgive, and release through sharing my personal stories and tools leveraged, I am equipped to offer guidance and coaching to support others who are searching to tap into purpose, find their peace, and start their own transformative journeys.

Use these takeaways and the questions that follow to embark on your own journey of self-discovery and resilience, drawing inspiration from my triumphs and lessons learned.

Pivotal Takeaways:

SILENT STRENGTH: Embrace the power of silence in moments of transformation. Sometimes, keeping pivotal decisions close can shield them from negativity and allow for introspection and divine guidance.

FAITHFUL OBEDIENCE: Trust in divine providence and step out in faith, even when conventional wisdom suggests otherwise. Obedience to a higher calling can lead to unexpected blessings and divine interventions.

RESILIENT PERSEVERANCE: Endure setbacks with unwavering resolve, maintaining faith in the face of adversity. Perseverance through financial strain and logistical challenges can ultimately lead to breakthroughs and fulfillment of purpose.

PURPOSEFUL REFLECTION: Reflect on personal experiences and recognize their alignment with your purpose. Sharing your stories can offer guidance and support to others embarking on their transformative journeys, fostering connection and inspiration.

Thoughts of Purpose:

To what decree can you hold your hope for something you are expecting?

Does manifestation of challenges bother you in the process of achieving that which you want?

What factors worked for or against your desires?

Scripture reflection: There is hope.
"Say I these things as a man? Or saith not the law the same also?"
(1Corinthians 9:8, KJV)

LAST WORD

IN A RECENT CONVERSATION WITH MY SISTER, she jokingly pointed out my penchant for always having snacks and food on hand, sparking a reflection on how past trauma influences our present behaviors. Growing up, amidst the chaos and uncertainty, food insecurity was constant reality that left me grappling with if we had enough for the next day. When I was on my own, my promise to myself was that I would never be without food. It wasn't merely about having snacks; it was about ensuring a sense of stability. I wanted my siblings to come to my house and know that I always had five to seven boxes of cereal, four to five jars of peanut butter and jelly, and cans of tuna. To outsiders, my stockpiles might seem excessive, but for me, it's a form of self-preservation stemming from the lack of food as a child, not hoarding.

But this conversation went deeper than just food; it unearthed the layers of coping mechanisms and behavioral patterns that we both carry as a result of our upbringing. It's about recognizing how our past experiences shape our present selves, sometimes in ways we never fully comprehend until we take a closer look.

Like my need to be in control goes beyond just micromanaging. It's rooted in a deep-seated belief that I had to maintain order and stability at all costs. The reality of it is that a child I was given the responsibilty to run a household, and care for my younger siblings in a chaotic environment. Being in control was a survival mechanism that served me well in childhood, but now it's a mixed bag, bringing both order and chaos into my life. It's a delicate balance, one that I'm still learning to navigate as I unravel the complexities of my past.

But recognizing these patterns is just the first step. The real work lies in untangling the trauma and redefining our relationship with ourselves and others. It's about accepting our flaws and imperfections, understanding that they are not weaknesses, but badges of resilience that made us stronger through years.

And so, as we journey through life, we must remember to look inward, to confront the demons of our past and find the courage to rewrite our own narratives. It's a journey of finding yourself and healing, and it takes patience, compassion, and, above all, grace.

So, to anyone out there dealing with the weight of their past, I encourage you to take a moment to pause, to reflect, and to recognize the strength inside you. You are not defined by your trauma. You are defined by your resilience, your courage, and your capacity to love. Embrace your uniqueness, embrace your journey, and above all, embrace yourself.

Today, I speak life into my spirit, affirming my worth, my value, and my inherent dignity. I am worthy. I am deserving. I am enough. I am healthy, wealthy, and wise. I am a wife, a purpose partner, and a child of God. And in that knowledge, I find the strength to keep growing, keep reflecting, and keep transforming, one step at a time.

ABOUT THE AUTHOR

DR. KELLY SERVES IN THE CAPACITY OF A SERVANT LEADER that uses her strategic expertise to guide others through their transformations by way of brainstorming, action planning, coaching, developing, and motivating other leaders. As a Humanitarian and Philanthropist, she always gives of herself to encourage, inspire and empower others to tap into and utilize their gifts from within.

Born in Newark, New Jersey, but raised in Plainfield, New Jersey, where she started to plan her life at a very early age of 13 when she realized that there had to be more in life than all the hurt, pain, abuse, deception, and death that she was witnessing and experiencing in her environment. She decided that she wanted more in life and sought an alternative educational opportunity. She decided she had to leave the environment that she knew, so she dropped out of high school and went to Job Corps Center in Callicoon, New York.

She graduated from that program at sixteen with her General Education Diploma. Kelly pushed forward and went to Business School and was blessed with an opportunity to work at Job Corp in Edison, NJ, before landing the start of her career in Management at AT&T/Lucent Technologies. She received a Master's Certification in Project Management from Steven Institute and a master's degree in health care. She continues to further her desires as an entrepreneur. She studied real estate and even went to Franklin Beauty Institute because of her love for hair, and the fashion industry.

In 1993 she started two companies, Klass and Elegance Productions and Ready for a Change. Klass & Elegance Productions held many events, particularly united and created a yearly network for over 300 family and friends and hair competitions within New Jersey and Pennslyvania. Her consulting company provided total makeovers to clients and her corporate colleagues, which included wardrobe shopping! By 1999, Arrington Enterprises was formed, and she owned and managed over six investment buildings.

Continuing to juggle working with and managing people with Engineering and MBA degrees at fortune 500 companies, even though she did not have a degree at all during this time, and she knows that it was the grace of God that qualified her. She learned very early that the highest level of intelligence is "common sense." Kelly started college part-time at Seton Hall University and after being in college for over ten years, in 2013, Kelly completed a Bachelor's of Science in Business Management, and a master's in Health Care. In 2021, she completed her doctorate in Strategic Leadership. She continues to use her 20-plus years of experience as an entrepreneur, real estate owner, project manager, visionary, and is now the "CTCO" Chief Transformation and Confidence Officer of her nonprofit organization called "Purpose 4 Living Inc" and her personal brand, "Dr. Kelly."

Dr. Kelly has been blessed with two sons, Akeem and Thornton, and a beautiful granddaughter, Jadyn Imani. In 2001, Kelly opened her home to PA-Monroe County Children and Youth as a "Safe House" for teenage boys. She has also been very active in a variety of corporate and community organizations. In 2008

Kelly organized a group of family and friends to participate in the North Carolina Signature Project to assist in building a 50-seat "outdoor" classroom for Partnership Alternative Academy School and was awarded a Forward-thinking Award from Blue Cross Blue Shield of North Carolina.

In 2013 Kelly started a Beating the Odds Scholarship program that has blessed many lives thus far, giving back to Job Corp students, and the first recipient was a 16-year-old young lady inspired to go back to further her education after overcoming human trafficking. In 2016, Kelly opened the doors of A House of Purpose Georgia, serving many through her Power of 7R's sessions – "Retreat, Reflection and Releasing allowing God to Re-new, Restore the mind with Resolutions and Readiness"
In 2019 through Purpose 4 Living Inc's partnership with the Rockdale County Jail RRSAT -Re-entry program Kelly served, Sheriff Levitt, as the Male and Female Transitional Thinking -Computer Training Coach.

Kelly continues to make her impact by being the first to introduce the significance of a cap and gown graduation; she received approval for funding and hosted the first Cap and Ground Graduation Ceremony in Rockdale County Jail in 2019. The ceremony continues today. Kelly was the first to receive the ACHII of Atlanta Servant Leader of the Year Award in 2019 and in 2023 Rockdale Commissioner recognized Dr. K as a Rockin Woman of Rockdale County for serving her community.

Today, this Corporate IT/Business Transformational Director, knows that her Purpose4Living is to be used as a vessel to share her story and tools she leveraged by coaching and strengthening "Transitional Thinking" that removes barriers like rejection, abandonment, Impostor Syndrome, and the importance of setting healthy boundaries which ultimately builds Confidence and Courage. Through Purpose 4 Living, Dr. K is committed to ignite the excellence within, which stimulates an execution mindset while she holds you accountable for what you say you want to accomplish, as they identify their Purpose4Living.

Prayerfully something you've read has made a difference in you?
Dr. Kelly would love to hear from you.
Please leave a review on Amazon or
Reach out to her on social media at:
Facebook @DrKelly A. Arrington-Wilkins

Instagram @ur2liveonpurpose

Contact Dr. K for coaching or facilitation of workshops or speaking engagements:
Dr. Kelly A. Arrington-Wilkins, DrSL, MHA, BSM, MCPM
Certified Transformational Confidence Coach
Visionary/Founder of Purpose 4 Living Inc.
Phone: (678) 408-1655
Email: info@Purpose4living.org or kellyarrington@purpose4living.org
Website: http://purpose4living.org

TESTIMONIALS

The name Kelly means warrior. However, I've composed the following as an acronym for who she really is:
K-Kinkeeping
E-Entrepreneur
L-Logistician
L-Liturgist
I've seen this enthusiastic, inquisitive young Christian grow into a positive force to be reckoned with. A Mature, seasoned, representative in Gods Kingdom. Kelly had a passion to discover where within lies my destiny and my purpose. She tapped into both through learning how "obedience is better than the sacrifice." She submitted to God's redirection of her future, recognizing and understanding. You must go through the process to get to her purpose. Kelly is a very astute, powerful, woman of God, my spiritual daughter.
— Dr. Lorretta V. Harris, Orlando, FL

Thank you Kelly Arrington for assisting me on discovering my hidden treasures that God has provided me to shine amongst me. Kelly has shown to me that everyone needs a co-pilot in their lives that has their best interest in heart. Sometimes man will go through life just drifting away; so it's imperative to have a life coach like you my sister to help strong and focused men and women like myself to bring everything past or present into perspective!!!
— Darryel Washington,Raleigh, NC

After being in my field of work for 20 plus years , the company that I had given everything to, changed direction and I was having a terrible time facing the unknown . Ms Kelly helped me face the emotional blocks that were keeping me from finding the next opportunity , with her help I was able to refocus , strategize and plot a new direction for my life. I am truly grateful for all her guidance in helping me move from a cloudy place.
— Ricky Guyton: Greenville, SC

Kelly Arrington-Wilkins, a woman of God, has been a remarkable coach, mentor, sister and friend. Her compelling life experience and testimony offer practical messages of healing, refuge, and encouragement. She embodies the essence of godly friendships, nurturing faith and providing valuable lessons for everyone she connects with. Kelly's wisdom and spiritual insight has been a major contribution to my life.

— Stephanie King, Birmingham, AL

Leadership is not a position I ever felt qualified for. But as she walks she gathers, I've been drawn to Kelly's light since I was a child and have observed her throughout the years. As I observed ,and admired, and listened, I retained. I retained the knowledge, the wisdom and the grace. I retained the ability to speak to others and their situation as she spoke to me and mine. Because of her I have been able to be the blessing that she was to me and walk women and men out of the same dark spaces that I knew well.
Because of her I was equipped!
  Equipped with the words, equipped with the motivation, equipped with the strategy, equipped with the prayer. Just yesterday I asked someone to find their WHY? Ironically I was asking myself the same question, and as I found my answer I pressed. The day following they quoted that they were finding their why as well.
  To have this type of impact that spreads across her path and touches so many people building a network unable to be seen by the naked eye but her words are spoken by many cross continental. Touch one you touch many. Kelly is a tree and her roots have spread and built a network that touch's other roots across the world.

— Yasmeen Davis, Destin, FL

After Having a conversation with Dr. K that lasted over an hour was truly inspirational for me. Meeting her for the first time, I was struck by the way she embodies the idea that it's not about how you start, but how you finish. Through our discussion, I was inspired by her unwavering trust in herself and the confidence she exudes. Dr. K's energy was so positive and judgment-free I could feel it through our entire interaction. It's clear that she uses her life experiences to motivate and uplift others on their own journeys. May God continue to bless Dr. K and all those she inspires.

— Jai Mykel, Houston, TX

Dr. Kelly has grown so much since elementary school to the fabulous women she is today. We didn't grow up with much, but Kelly had the confidence of knowing she wasn't going to take any mess from anyone and wanted more out of life. She is a true friend that I can count on and know that she has my back. Kelly stood out among her peers. She was motivated and eager to strive for the best. Over the years I've witnessed her pour into people and do better and better even when she had some bumps in the road, she made it look flawless but I'm sure it was God and hard work. Like they say it takes faith and hard work to get want you want out of life and where we came from, she did both.

— Sergeant Bilal, Plainfield, NJ/GA

FROM PRESCOTT PLACE TO PURPOSE

P- Prayer   P-Purpose
R-Resilient   U-Universe
E-Endured   R-Renewed
S-Sustained   P-Progress
C-Confident   O-One-of-a-kind
O-Overcomer   S-Successful
T-Transformative   E-Embraced the lessons
T-Tenacious

Kelly was one of a few of us that "GOT AWAY" and accomplished what many could only imagine). You Beat The Odds ~ Jonah 1: 17

—Your Childhood Righteous Sister Kasmir (Keisha Battle)

Made in the USA
Columbia, SC
02 May 2025

57279615R00046